Albania
Coloring The World

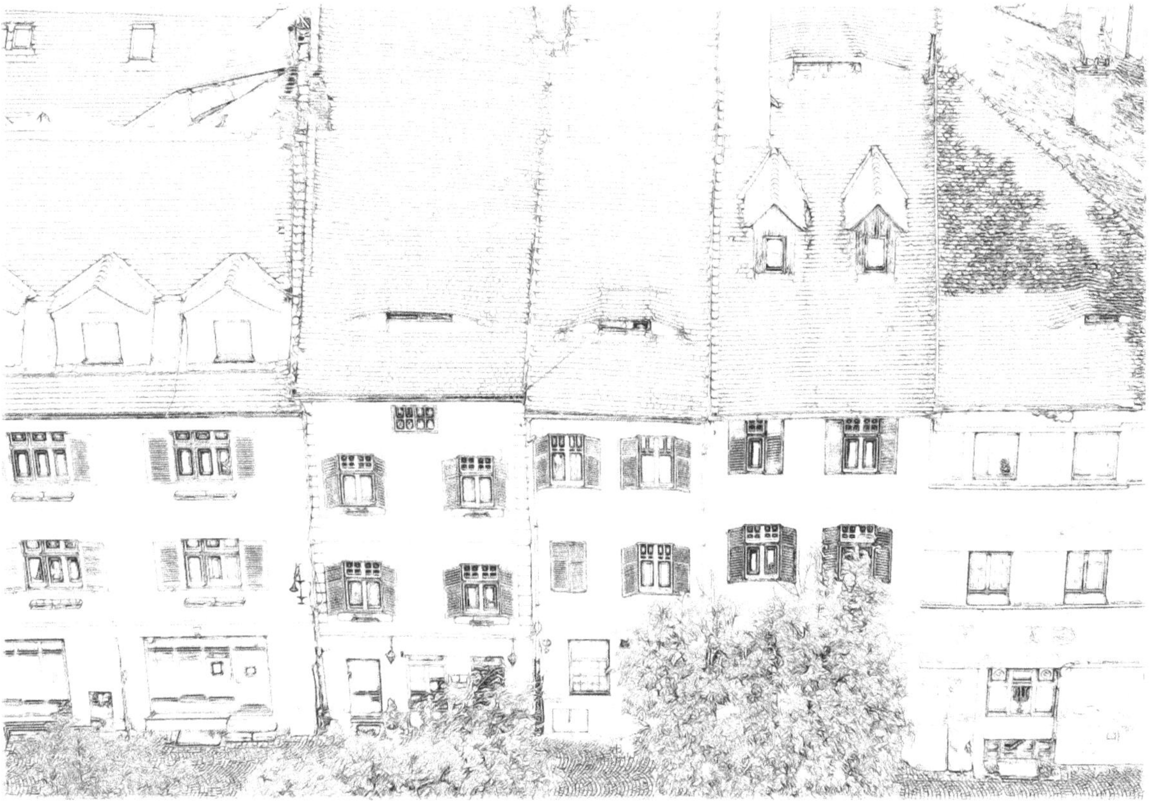

Anthony Hutzler

Sketch Coloring Book

Published July 2016

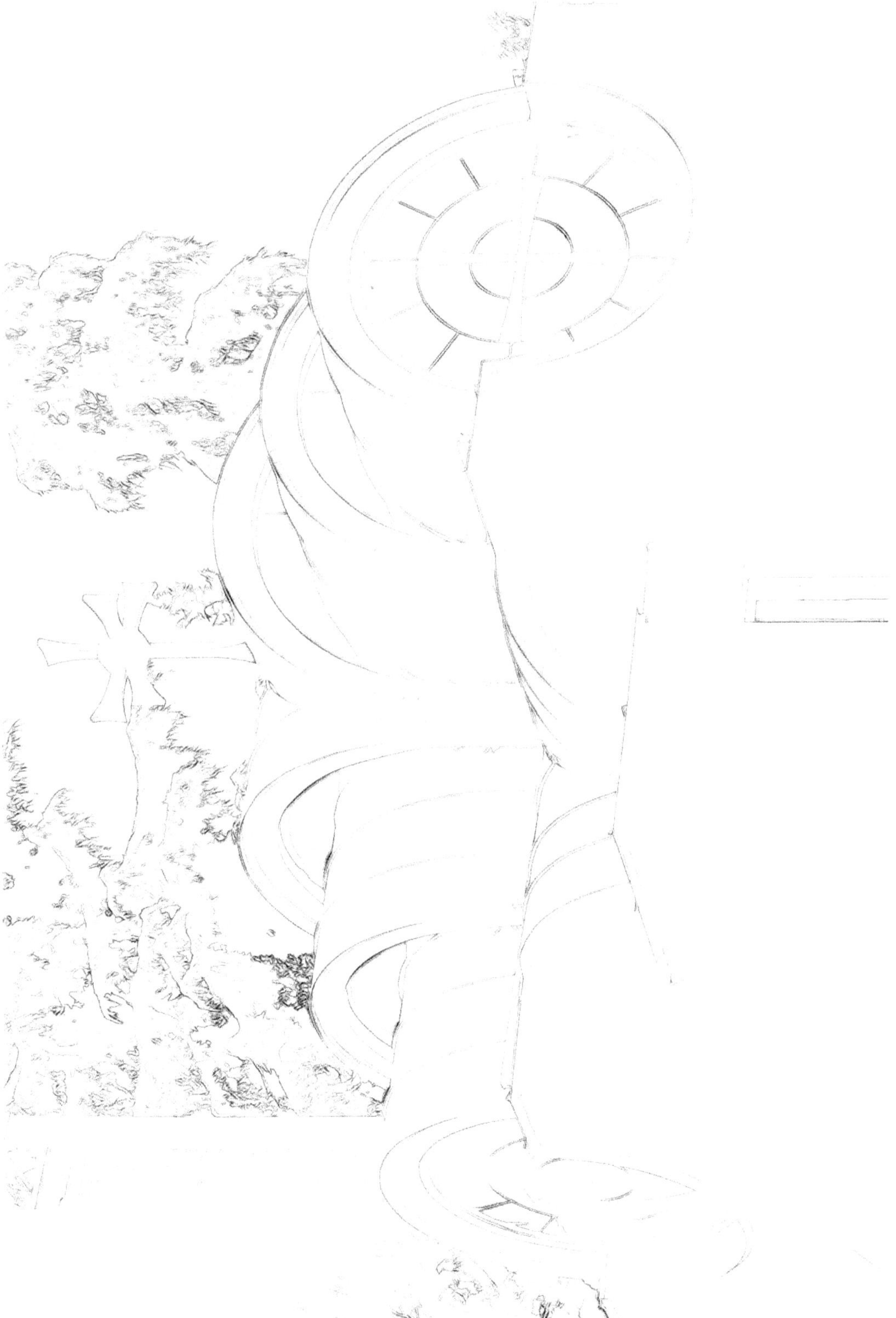

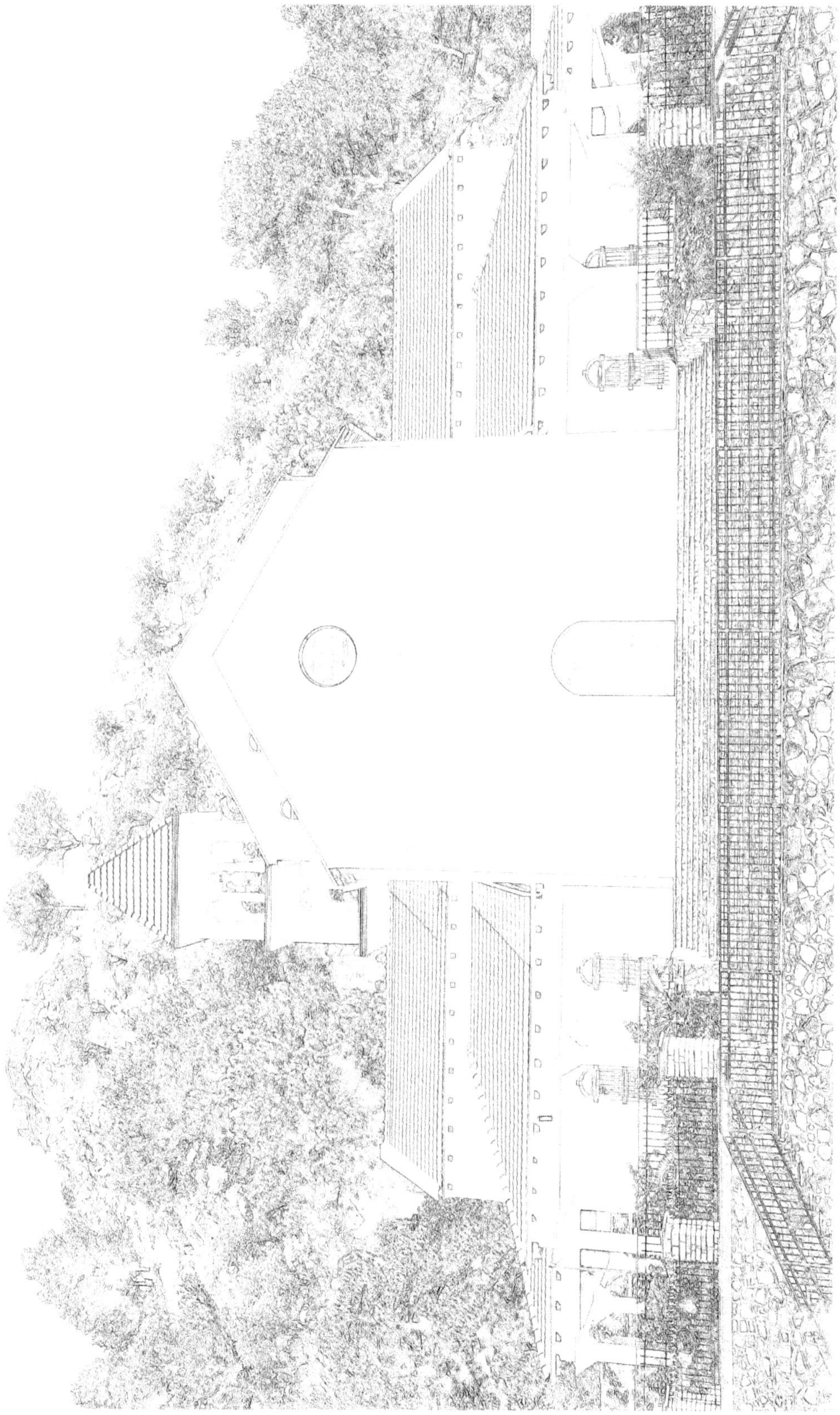

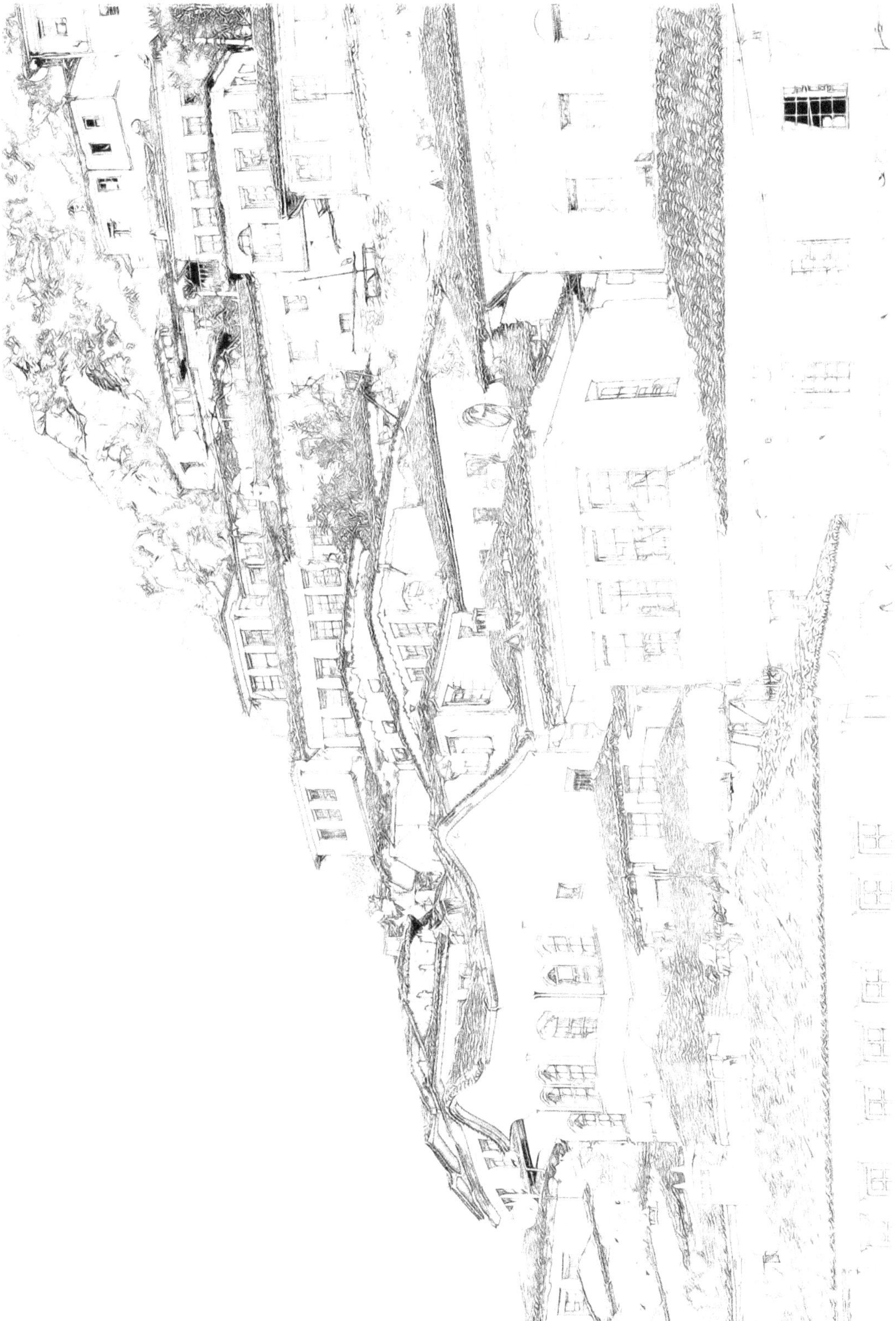

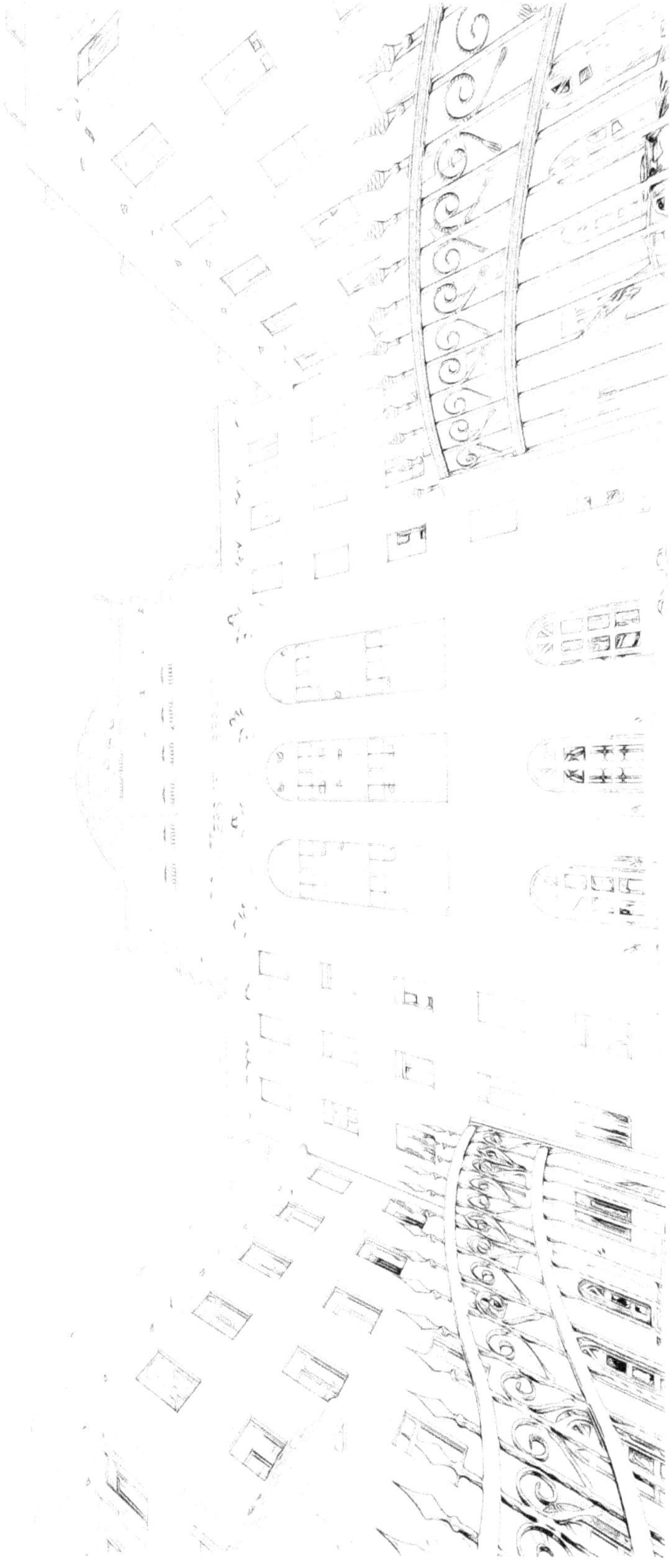

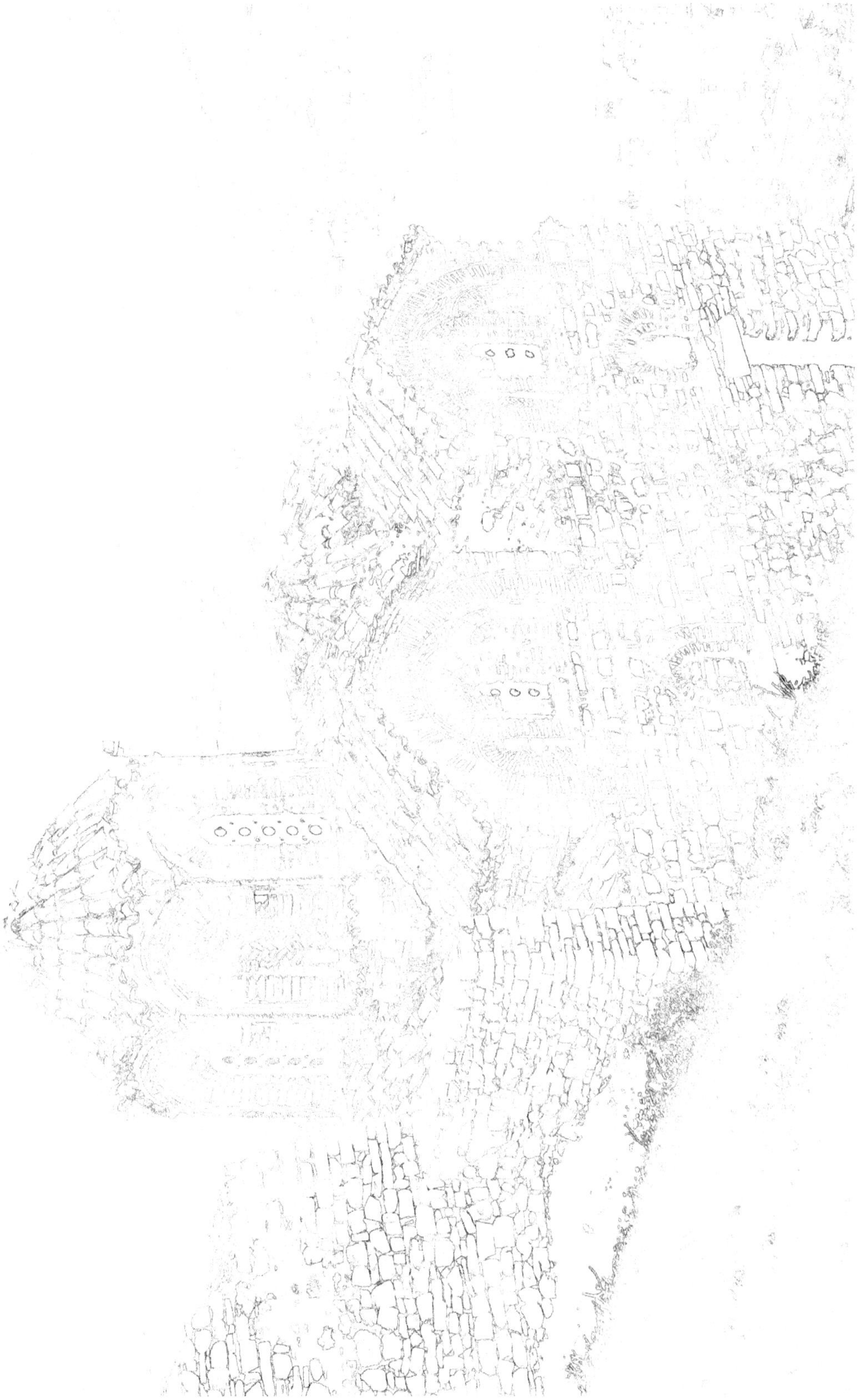

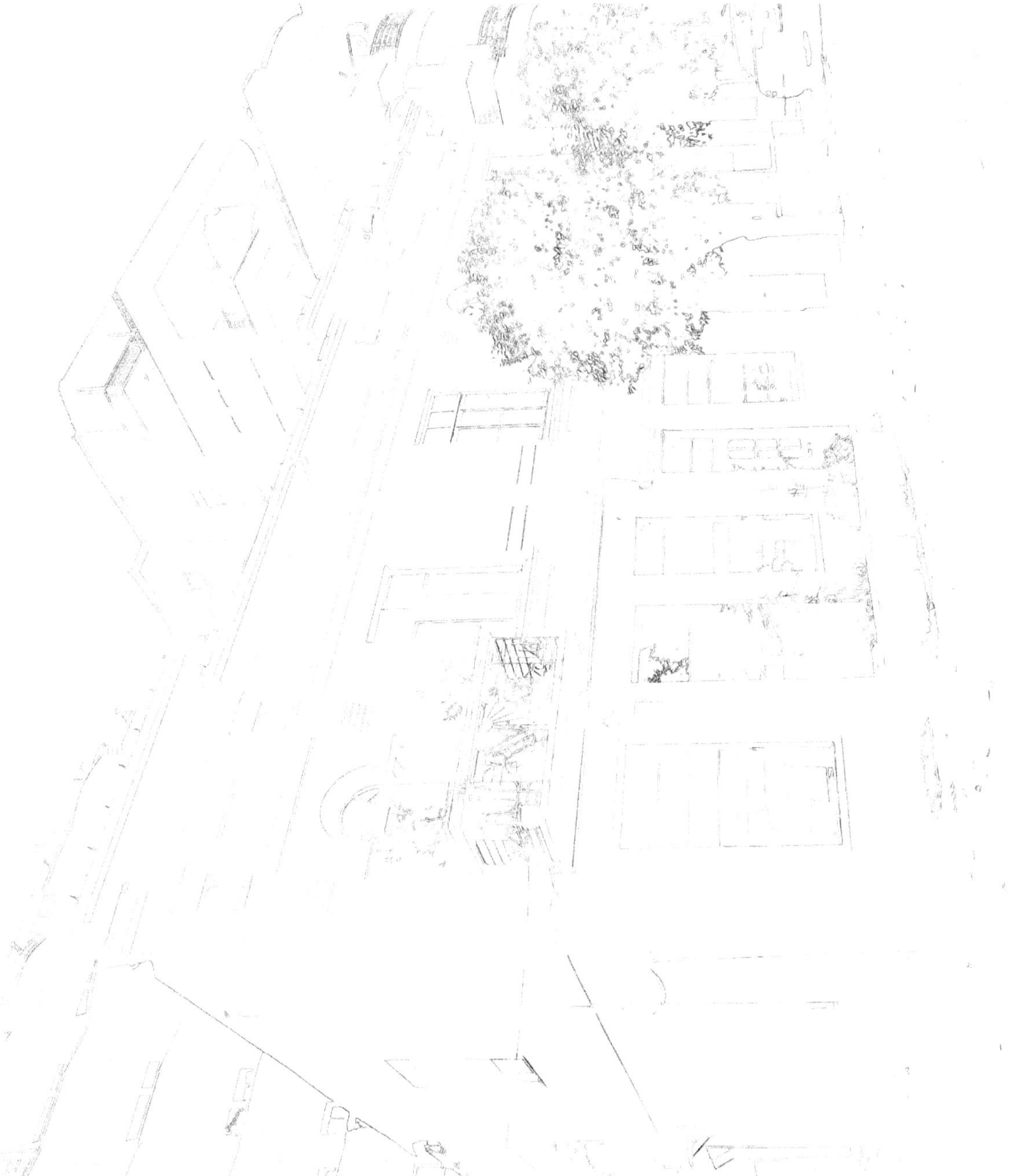

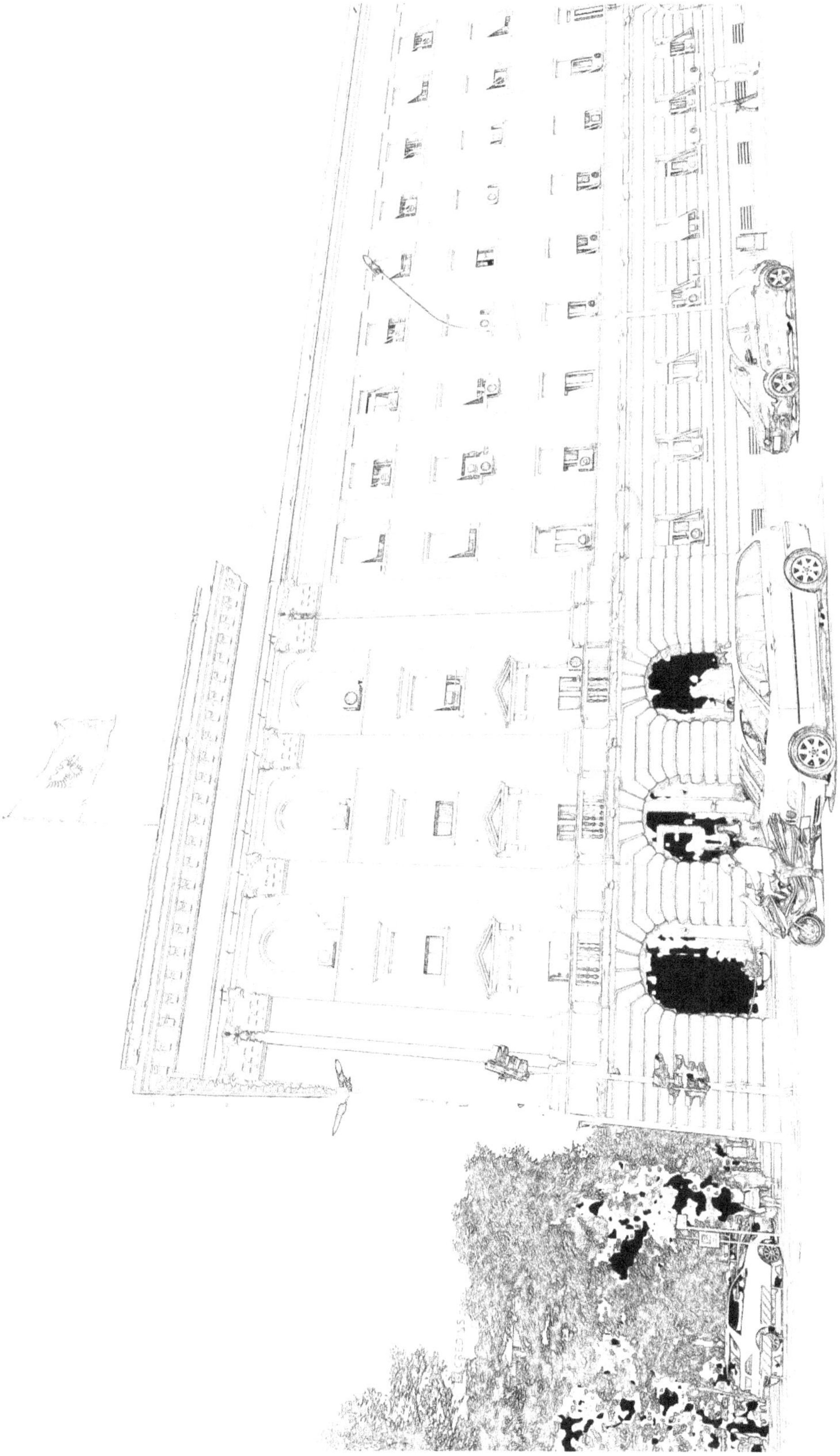

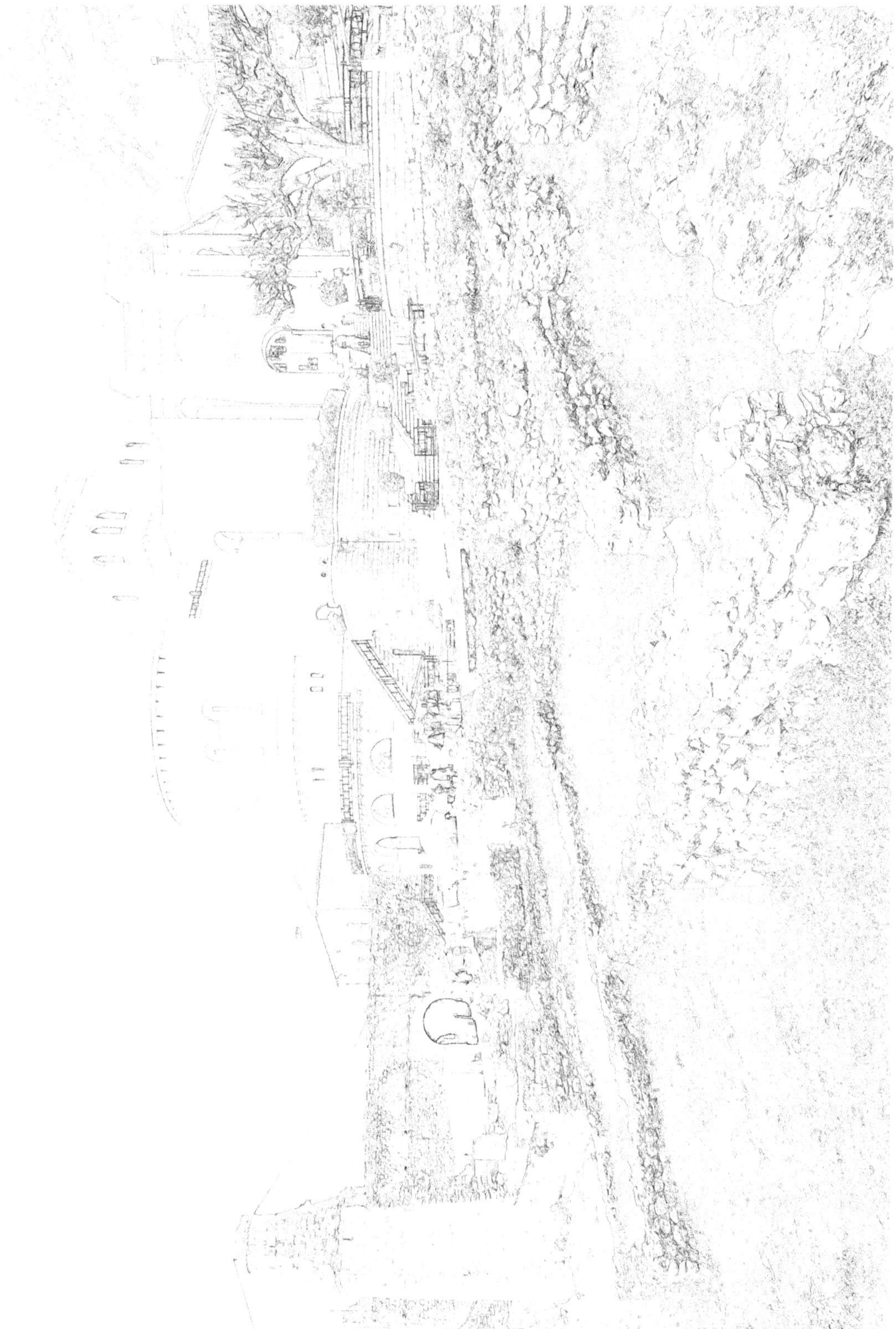

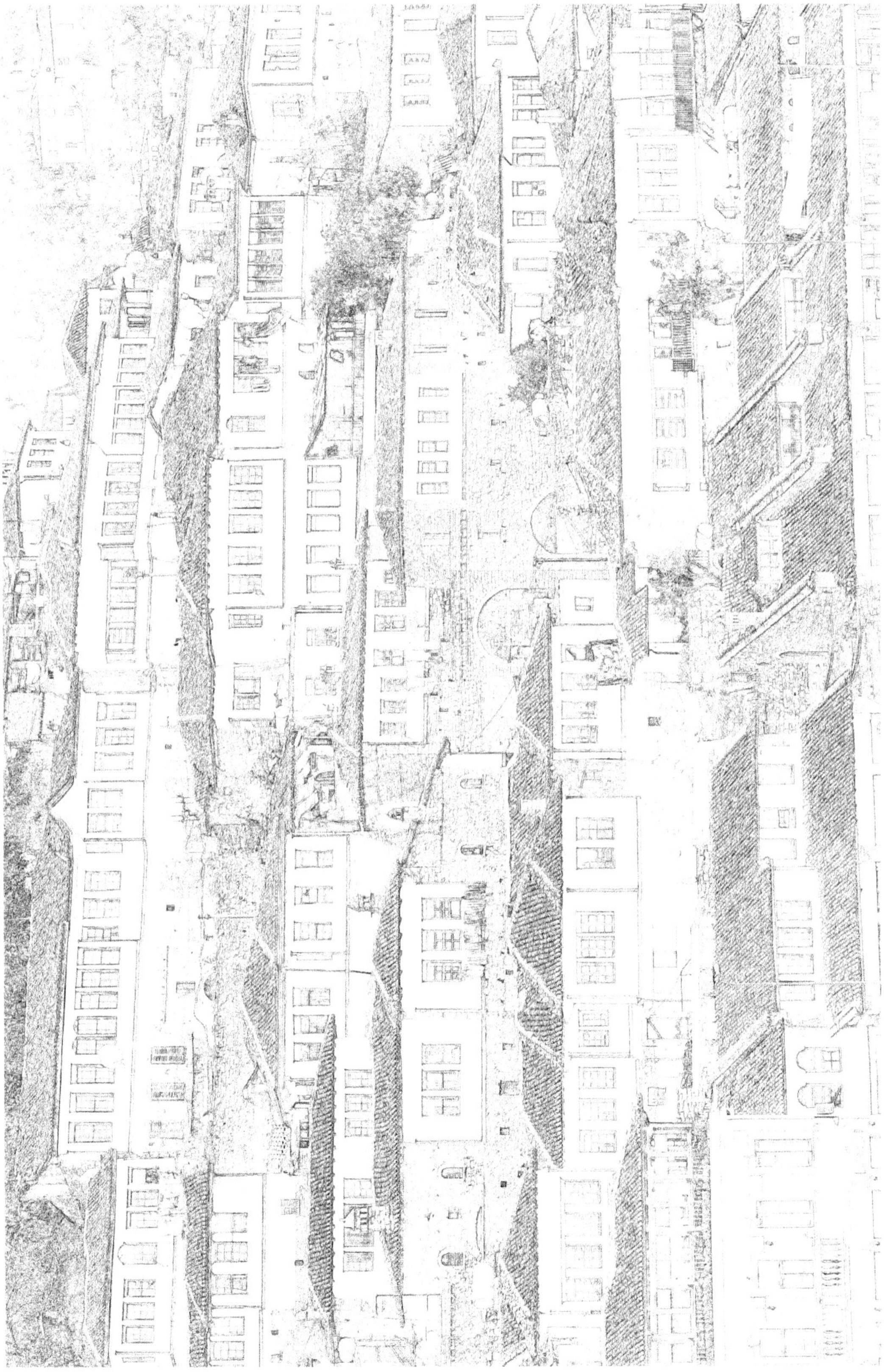

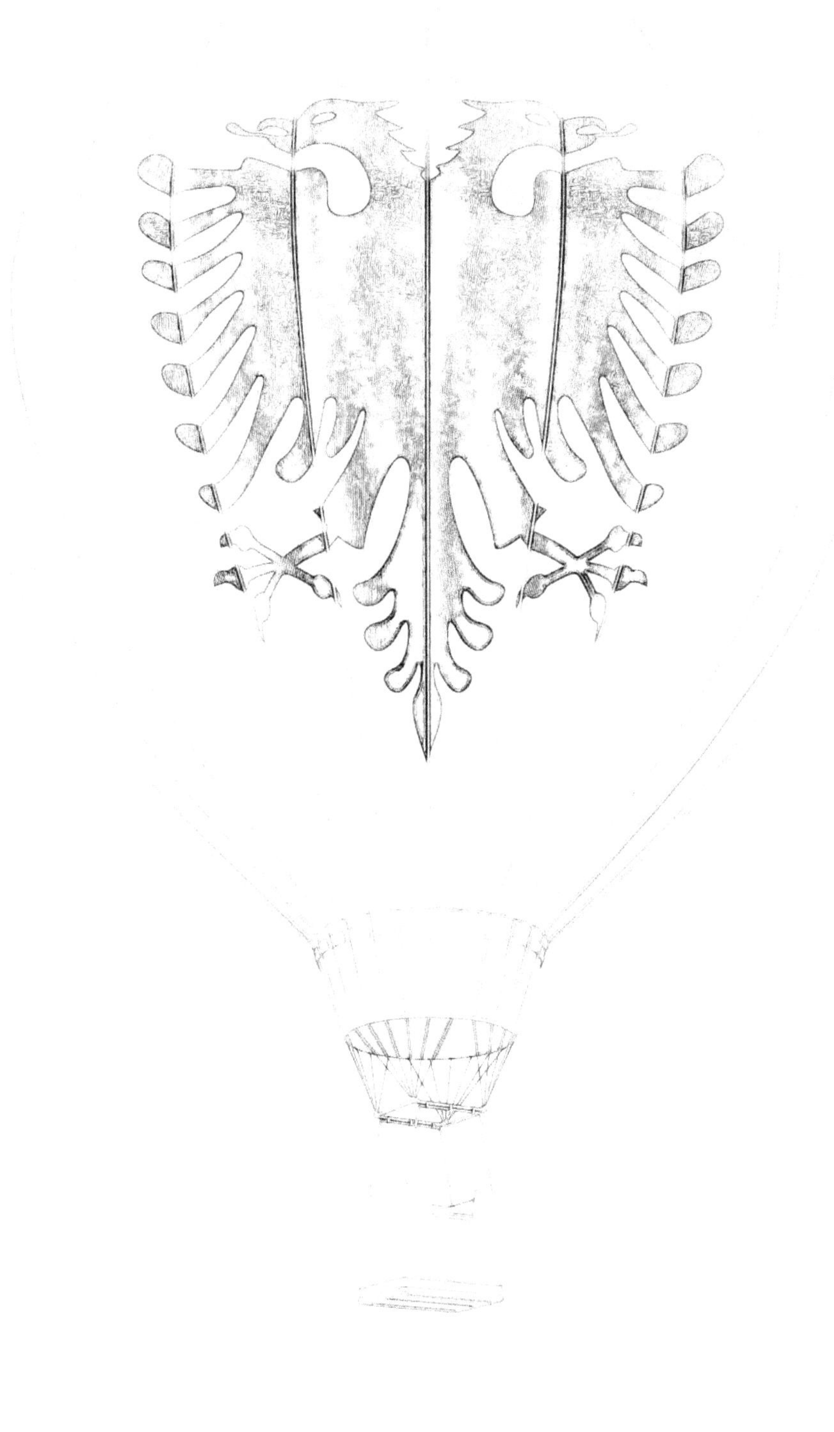

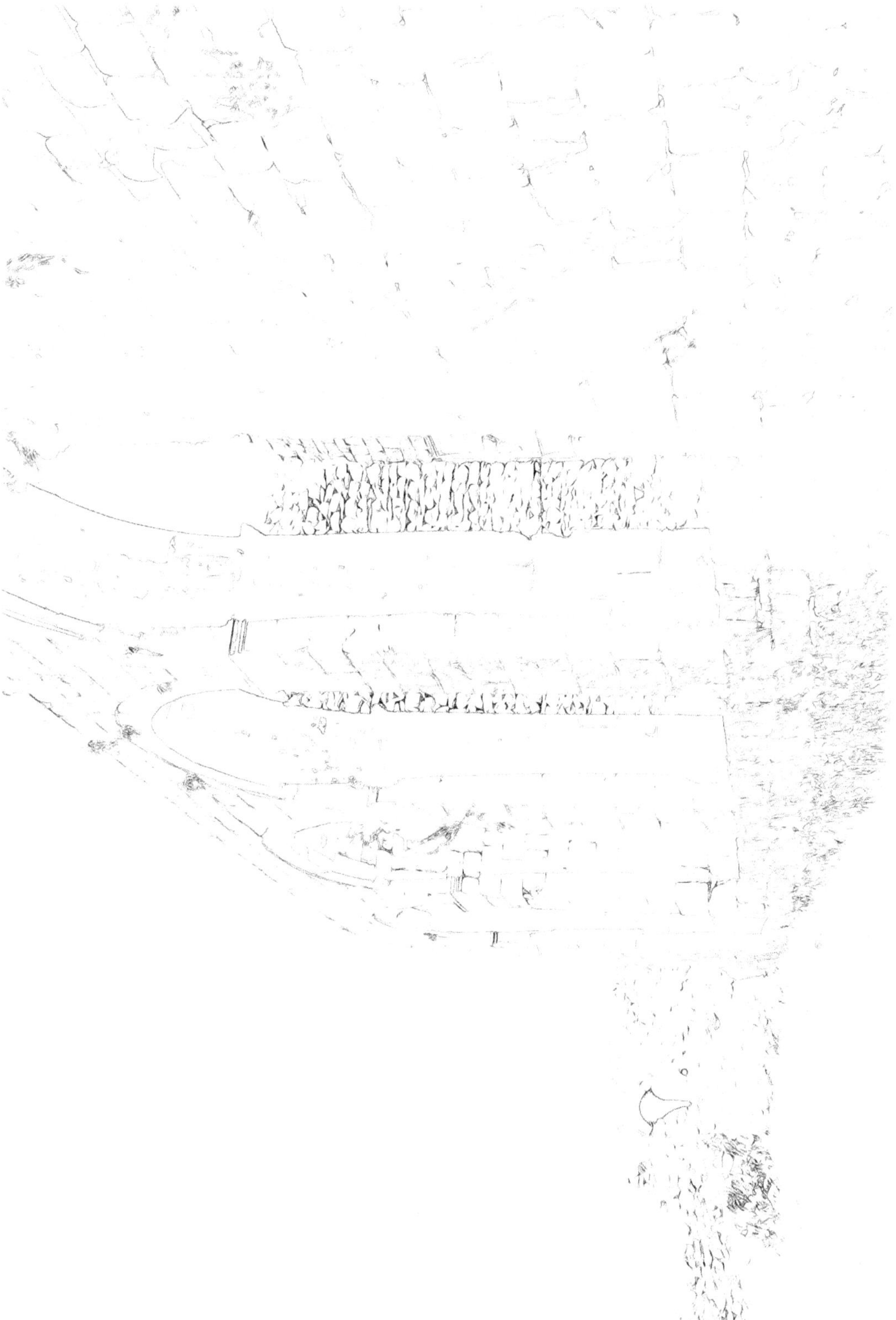

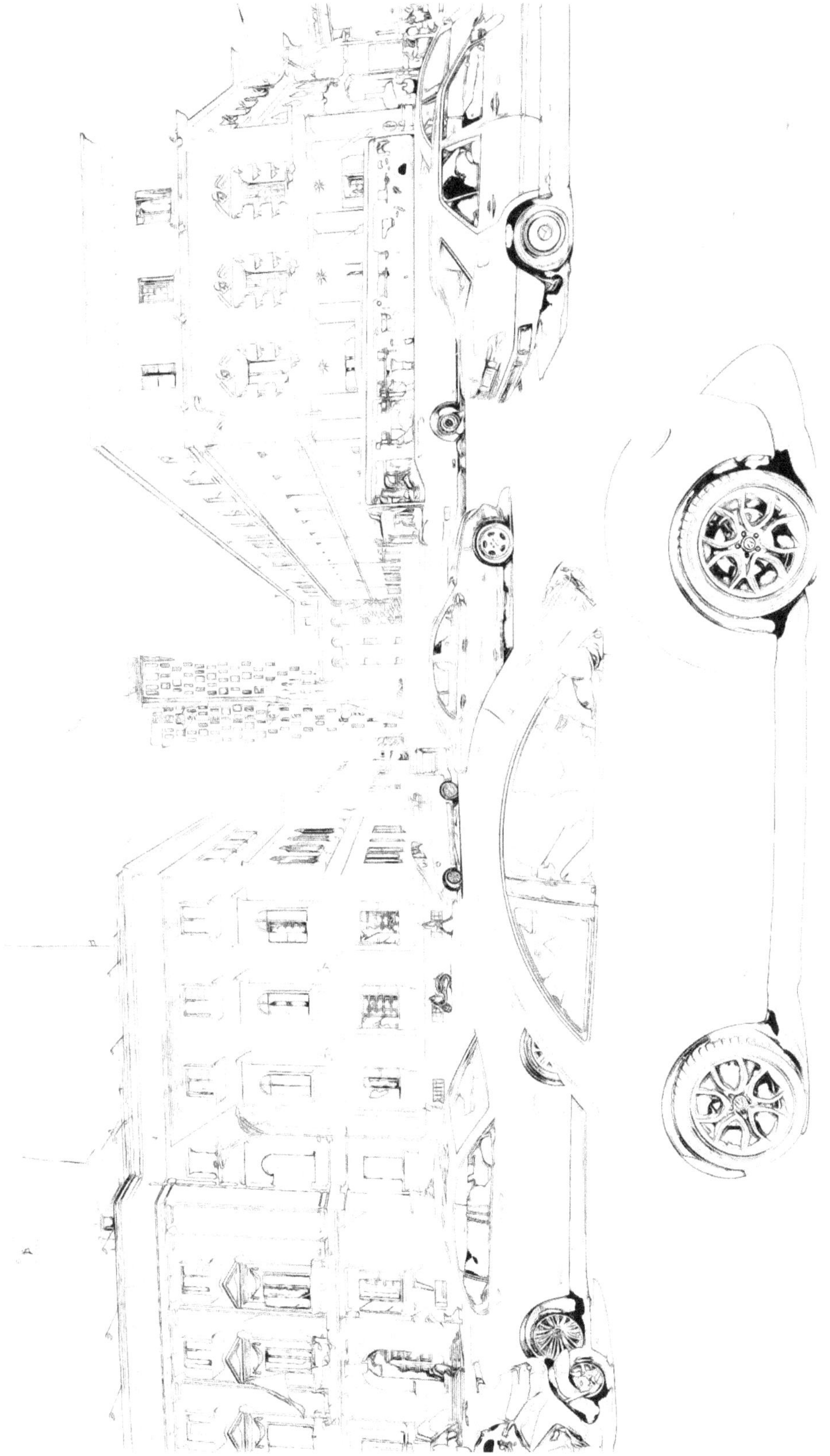

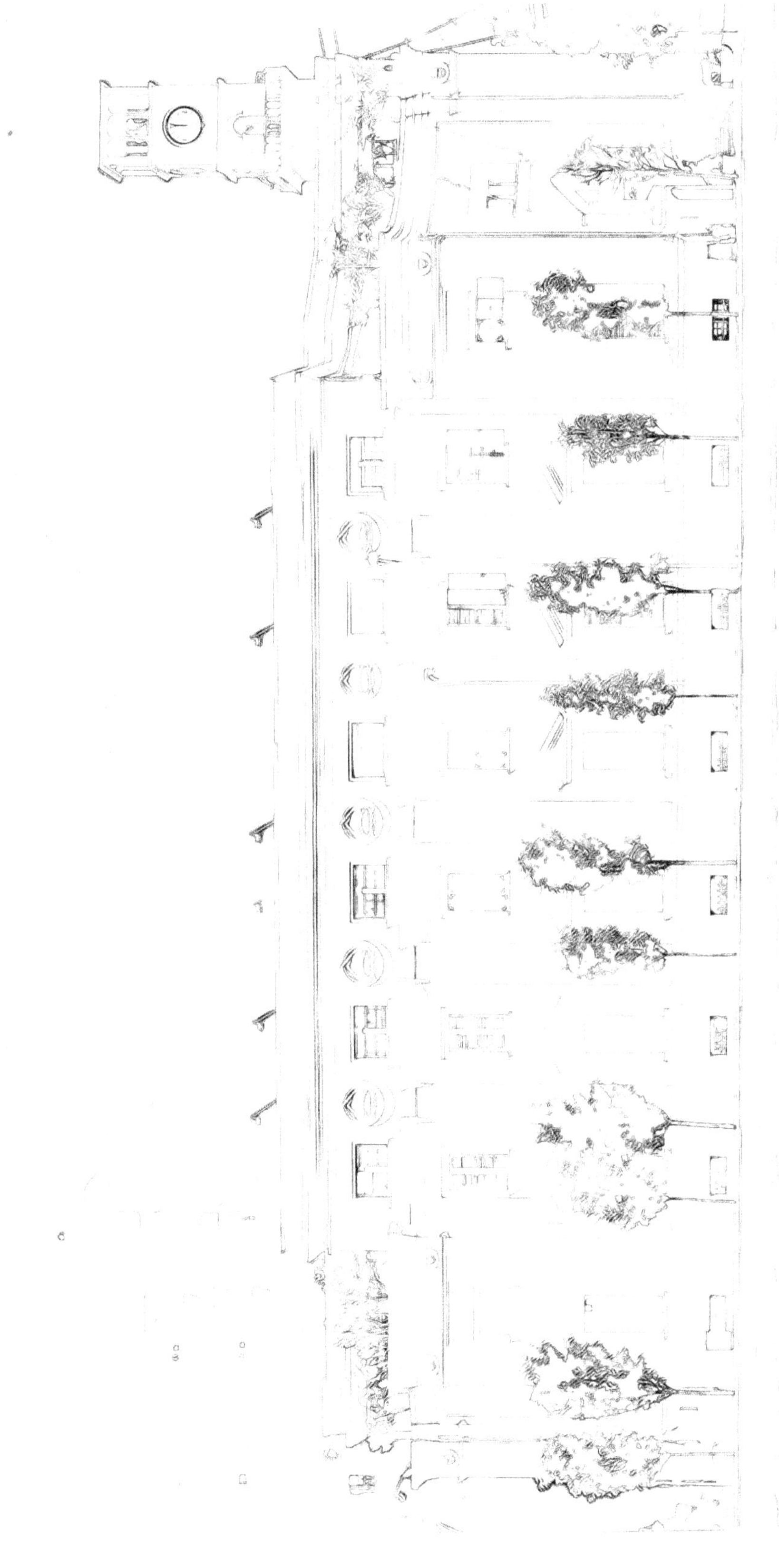

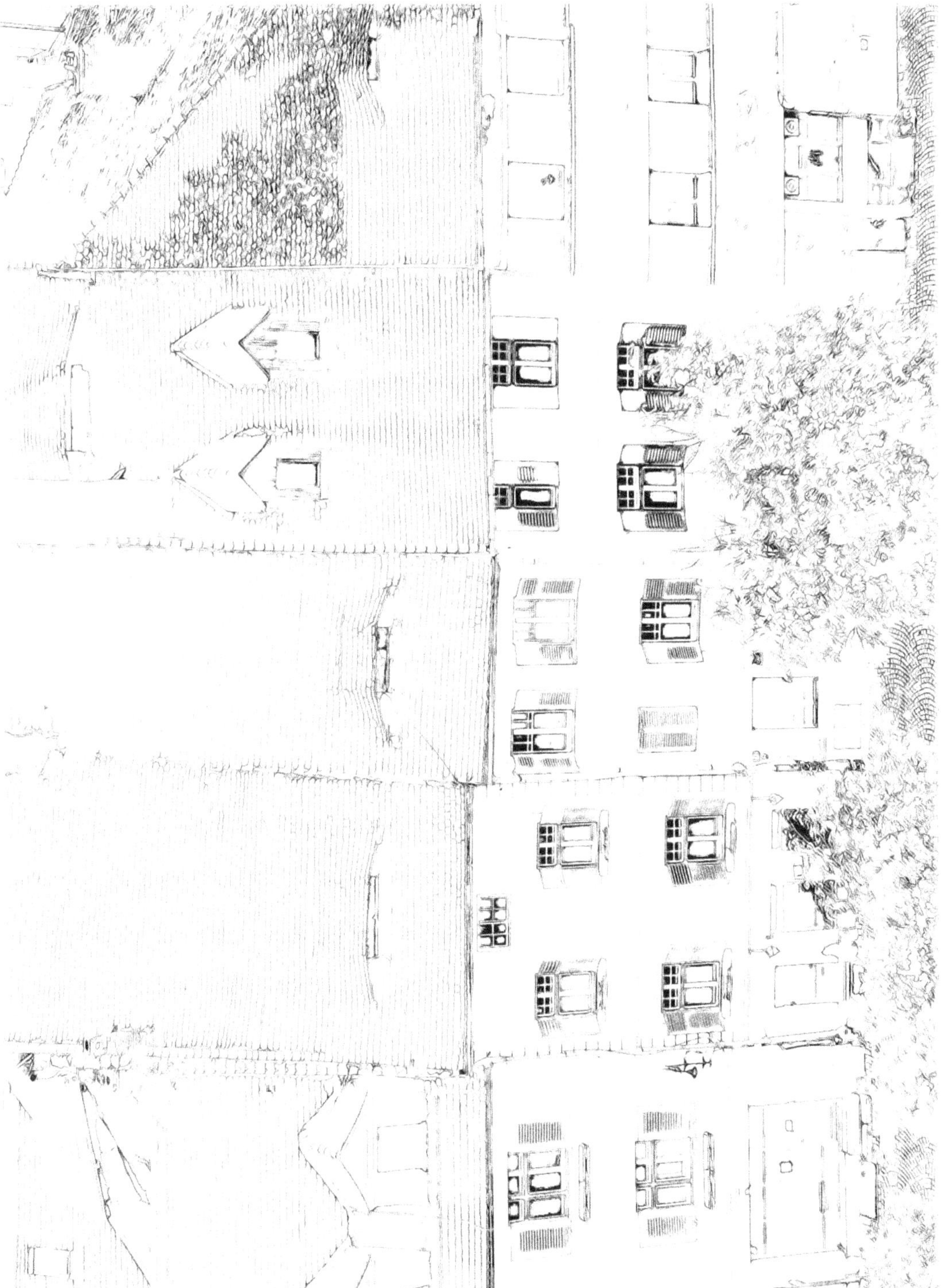

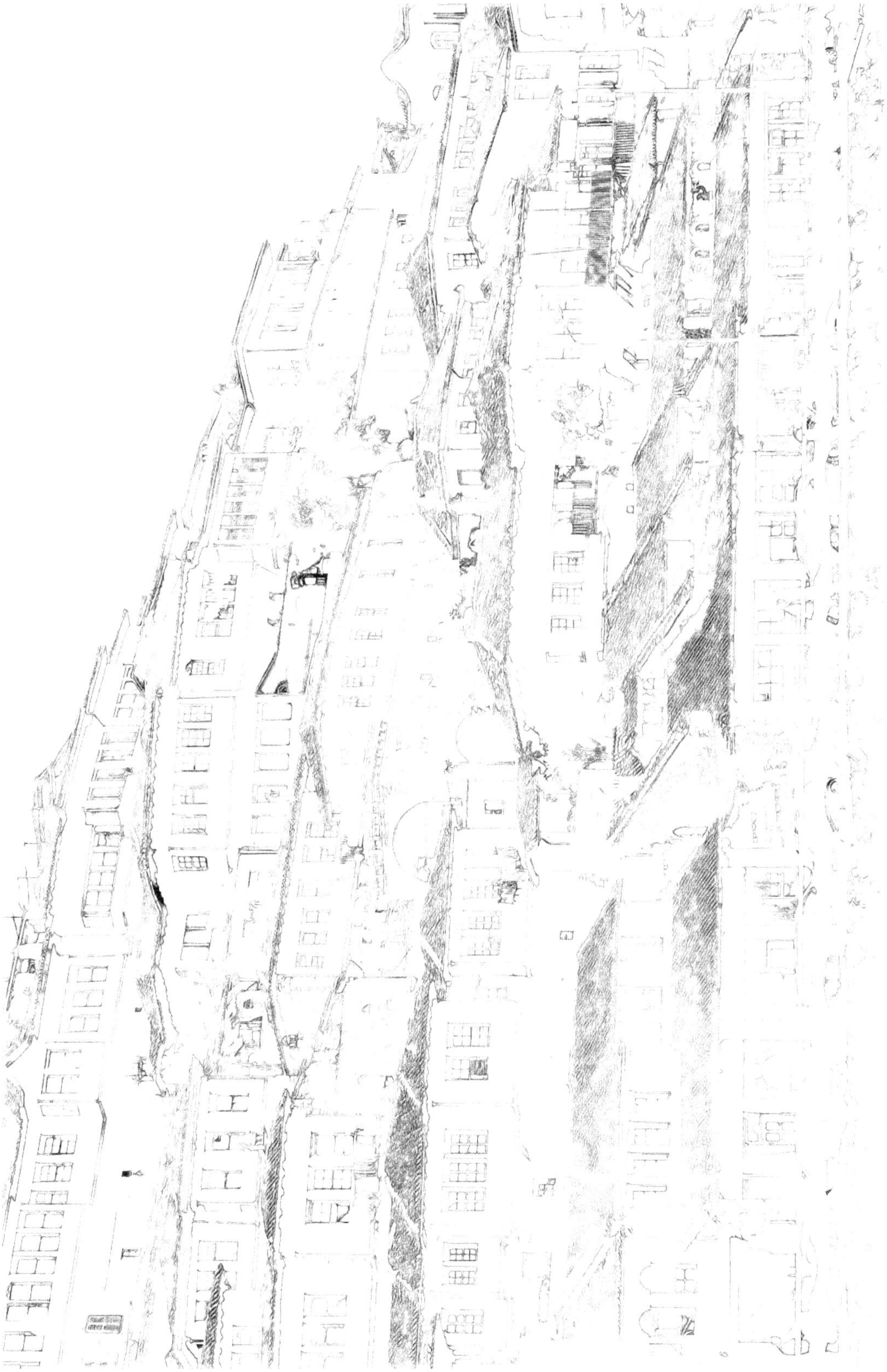

Picture Guide for this book : http://bit.ly/Albania_Coloring

Don't Miss Another our Books.

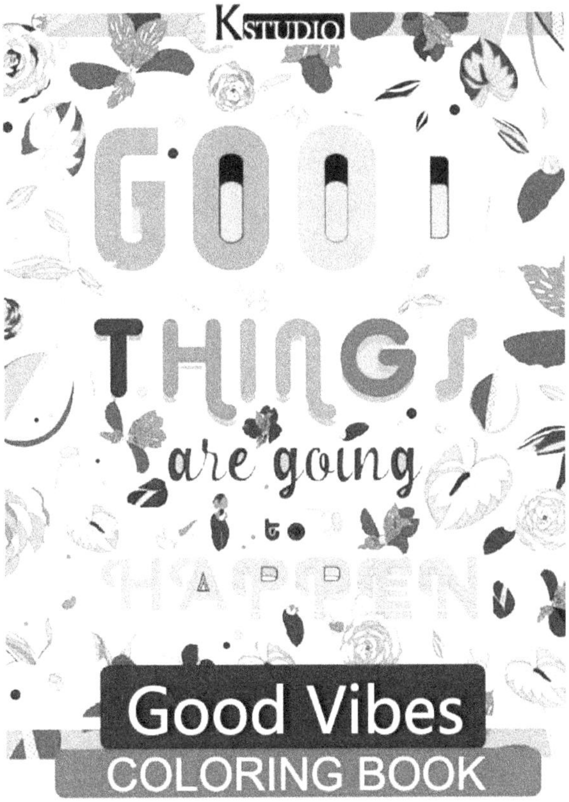

http://bit.ly/good_vibes_1

ISBN : 1530381223
(Use this ISBN for searching on amazon.com)

www.ingramcontent.com/pod-product-compliance
Lightning Source LLC
Chambersburg PA
CBHW081128180526
45170CB00008B/3046
* 9 7 8 1 5 3 9 6 8 7 7 2 6 *